COOKIES
for youthful appetites

SO-DOP-652

Printed in the United States of America

ISBN 1-56383-008-6

TABLE OF CONTENTS

DROP COOKIES

BASIC COOKIE MIX

1 C. white sugar	1 tsp. soda
1 C. brown sugar	½ tsp. baking powder
2¼ C. flour	1 C. shortening
1 tsp. salt	3 C. rolled oats

Mix above ingredients well. This makes 8 cups of mix. This may be kept in refrigerator and used later. For 1½ to 2 dozen small cookies: 1 egg, 1 teaspoon vanilla and 2 cups cookie mix. May add nuts, raisins, coconut or chocolate chips. Drop by teaspoon on lightly greased cookie sheet. Bake 400° 8 to 10 minutes.

DROP SUGAR COOKIES

½ C. butter
½ C. shortening
1 C. sugar
2 eggs

2 tsp. vanilla
2½ C. flour, not sifted
¾ tsp. baking powder
1 tsp. salt

Preheat oven to 350°. Cream butter and shortening. Add sugar gradually. Add unbeaten eggs, one at a time. Add vanilla and dry ingredients. Drop on greased cookie sheet. Flatten with a glass dipped in sugar. Bake at 350° for 10 minutes. Yield: 5 dozen.

SOUR CREAM SUGAR COOKIES

½ C. shortening
2 C. sugar
3 eggs
1 C. sour cream
½ tsp. soda
1 tsp. baking powder

½ tsp. salt
1 tsp. vanilla <u>or</u>
 1 tsp. lemon extract
¼ C. black walnuts
3½ C. flour

Preheat oven to 375°. Blend shortening and sugar. Add eggs. Add sour cream, then blend in rest of ingredients. Add a pinch of sugar to top of each cookie before baking. Bake for 8 to 10 minutes. Yield: 5 dozen.

SOUR CREAM SOFTIES

3 C. sifted flour
1 tsp. salt
½ tsp. baking powder
½ tsp. baking soda
½ C. butter or margarine

1½ C. sugar
2 eggs
1 tsp. vanilla
1 C. (8 oz.) carton dairy
  sour cream
Cinnamon-sugar

Preheat oven to 400°. Measure flour, salt, baking powder and soda into a sifter. Cream butter or margarine with sugar until well blended. Beat in eggs and vanilla. Sift in flour mixture, adding alternately with sour cream and blending well to make a thick batter. Drop by tablespoons 4" apart on greased cookie sheet. Spread in 2" rounds. Spread with cinnamon-sugar. Bake for 12 minutes.

4

BUTTER COOKIES

1½ C. butter
¾ C. powdered sugar
½ tsp. salt

1 C. finely chopped
 utmeats
2 C. flour

Preheat oven to 350°. Cream the butter and powdered sugar. Add salt and beat well. Add chopped nuts and sifted flour. Mix well. Drop by teaspoons on greased cookie sheet. Bake for 12 to 15 minutes. While still warm, roll in granulated sugar. Yield: 6 dozen.

GINGER CREAMS

¼ C. shortening
½ C. sugar
1 egg
⅓ C. molasses
2 C. sifted flour
½ tsp. soda

½ tsp. salt
1 tsp. ginger
½ tsp. cinnamon
½ tsp. cloves
½ C. water

Preheat oven to 400°. Cream shortening and sugar. Beat in egg. Stir in molasses. Sift dry ingredients. Add alternately with water. Drop from teaspoon onto greased cookie sheet. Bake about 8 minutes. While slightly warm, frost with confectioner's icing. Yield: 3 dozen.

AMBROSIA DROP COOKIES

½ C. butter or oleo
½ C. sugar
1 egg
1¼ C. flour
½ tsp. baking powder

½ tsp. salt
1 T. grated orange rind
1 C. chopped pecans
1 C. flaked coconut
Whole pecans

Preheat oven to 375°. Cream butter. Add sugar gradually and cream until light and fluffy. Add egg and beat well. Mix in dry ingredients (which have been sifted together) and then stir in orange rind, nuts and coconut. Drop on greased cookie sheet, press a whole pecan onto the center of each cookie and bake for 12 to 14 minutes. Yield: 3 dozen.

FROSTED RAW APPLE COOKIES

½ C. lard
1½ C. brown sugar
1 egg
¼ C. milk
1 tsp. vanilla
1 C. grated raw apples
1 C. raisins
1 C. walnuts

2 C. flour
1 tsp. baking powder
½ tsp. soda
½ tsp. salt
½ tsp. nutmeg
½ tsp. cinnamon
¼ tsp. cloves

Preheat oven to 350°. Cream lard and sugar. Mix well. Add eggs and vanilla. Sift dry ingredients. Add ½ to creamed mixture. Add apples, raisins, nuts and milk. Mix well. Add remaining flour mixture. Mix well. Drop by teaspoonfuls on greased cookie sheet. Bake for 12 minutes. Frost with powdered sugar icing.

8

CHOCOLATE SUNDAE COOKIES

1½ C. flour
½ tsp. soda
½ tsp. salt
⅔ C. brown sugar
½ C. shortening
1 egg

¼ C. maraschino cherry juice
2 T. milk
2 sqs. melted unsweetened chocolate
½ C. walnuts, chopped
¼ C. chopped maraschino cherries

Preheat oven to 350°. Sift flour, soda and salt. Set aside. Add sugar gradually to shortening, creaming well. Blend in unbeaten egg. Beat well. Stir in half the dry ingredients. Add maraschino cherry juice and milk, then stir in remaining dry ingredients. Mix well. Blend in chocolate, nuts and cherries. Drop by rounded teaspoonfuls on ungreased baking sheets. Bake for 12 to 15 minutes. Cut 18 marshmallows in half. Place cut side down on hot cookie. Cool on rack. Frost with chocolate powdered sugar frosting. Top each cookie with a nut.

9

BACHELOR BUTTONS

1 stick margarine
¾ C. brown sugar
1 egg
2⅓ C. flour
1 tsp. baking soda

⅛ tsp. salt
1 C. shredded coconut
¼ C. chopped walnuts
½ C. chopped maraschino
 cherries

Preheat oven to 350°. Cream margarine, add sugar and cream well. Beat egg and add to sugar mixture. Add coconut, walnuts and cherries. Blend well. Mix flour, baking soda and salt and add to first mixture very gradually. If mixture seems a little too thick, add a few drops of milk. Drop on greased baking sheet. Bake about 15 to 20 minutes. Yield: 3 dozen.

COFFEE COOKIES

1½ C. brown sugar	1 tsp. cinnamon
1 C. shortening (half oleo)	½ tsp. cloves
3 eggs	½ tsp. allspice
1 tsp. soda	½ tsp. salt
4 T. hot coffee	1 C. chopped nuts
2½ C. flour	1 C. seedless raisins

Preheat oven to 375°. Cream shortening and sugar. Add eggs, one at a time, beating well. Dissolve soda in strong, hot coffee (one tablespoon instant coffee to four tablespoons of hot water). Add soda and coffee to first mixture. Beat well. Sift, measure and mix dry ingredients together. Add to other mixture gradually. Add nuts and raisins. Drop by teaspoon on greased cookie sheet 2" apart. Bake for 10 minutes. Frost with Mocha Icing when cooled. Yield: 5 dozen.

COCONUT MACAROONS

1 can (1⅓ C.) Eagle Brand
condensed milk

6 C. shredded coconut
2 tsp. vanilla

Preheat oven to 350°. Blend milk, coconut and vanilla. Drop by teaspoonfuls about 1" apart on well greased cookie sheet. Bake until delicate brown, 8 to 10 minutes. Remove from pan at once. A whole or half candied cherry may be place in the center of each cookie before baking. Yield: 5 dozen.

COCONUT KISSES

2 egg whites
1 C. sugar
½ tsp. vanilla

2 C. cornflakes
1-3½ oz. can flaked coconut
½ C. chopped nuts

Preheat oven to 350°. Beat egg whites and dash of salt until foamy. Gradually add sugar and beat until stiff. Add vanilla. Fold in remaining ingredients. Drop from teaspoons onto well greased cookie sheet. Bake about 20 minutes. Remove cookies immediately. If they stick to pan, return to oven to soften. If desired, spiral melted unsweetened chocolate (1-1 ounce square melted with ½ teaspoon shortening) atop cookies. Yield: 2 dozen.

13

CHOCOLATE CHIP COOKIES

1 C. oleo
1 C. white sugar
1 C. brown sugar
2 eggs
1 tsp. soda

2½ C. flour
1 tsp. vanilla
½ C. nuts
1-6 oz. pkg. chocolate chips

Preheat oven to 325°. Cream sugars and oleo together. Add eggs and vanilla. Sift dry ingredients and add to mixture. Add nuts and chocolate chips. Bake.

CHOCOLATE CHIPS OATMEAL COOKIES

1-12 oz. pkg. chocolate chips
3 C. flour
3 tsp. baking powder
1 tsp. salt
3 C. rolled oats
1 C. + 2 T. shortening

1½ C. brown sugar
3 eggs, unbeaten
1 C. nuts
½ C. milk
1 T. vanilla
¾ C. raisins (optional)

Sift flour, salt and baking powder together. Then combine the rolled oats. Cream shortening and sugar. Add eggs, one at a time. Beat thoroughly. Add chocolate chips, nuts, raisins, milk and vanilla. Bake for 10 to 12 minutes. Yield: 8 dozen.

15

CHOCOLATE CHIP CREAM COOKIES

½ C. butter
1½ C. packed brown sugar
2 eggs
1 tsp. vanilla
2½ C. sifted flour
1 tsp. baking soda
½ tsp. baking powder
½ tsp. salt
1 C. plain yogurt
12 oz. pkg. semi-sweet chocolate chips
1 C. chopped nuts

Preheat oven to 375°. Cream butter and sugar. Beat until light and fluffy. Beat in eggs and vanilla. Sift dry ingredients. Add to creamed mixture alternately with yogurt, beginning and ending with dry ingredients. Stir in chocolate chips and nuts. Drop by teaspoonfuls on greased baking sheet. Bake for 10 to 12 minutes. Remove from cookie sheet immediately, cool. Yield: 7½ dozen.

CHOCOLATE CHIP BROWN SUGAR COOKIES

¼ lb. oleo or butter
1 C. brown sugar
2 eggs
⅓ C. milk
2 C. flour

2 tsp. baking powder
1 tsp. salt
1 C. chocolate chips
1 C. walnuts or pecans

Preheat oven to 400°. Combine butter and sugar. Add eggs, one at a time. Mix thoroughly. Add dry ingredients with milk. Add chocolate chips and nuts. Drop on ungreased cookie sheet. Bake 15 minutes. Yield: 3 dozen.

CHOCOLATE CHIP SAND TARTS

1 C. butter	1¼ C. sugar
⅛ tsp. salt	1 egg
1 tsp. vanilla	2 C. sifted flour
½ tsp. almond extract	1-6 oz. pkg. (1 C.) chocolate chips

Preheat oven to 350°. Combine and blend well butter, salt, vanilla and almond extract. Beat sugar in gradually. Beat in egg. Stir in flour. Add chocolate chips. Drop on ungreased cookie sheet. Bake 15 minutes. Yield: 6 dozen.

CHOCOLATE CRISP BRAN BUD COOKIES

1 C. butter or oleo
1½ C. sugar
2 eggs
1 tsp. vanilla
2 C. flour

½ tsp. soda
½ tsp. salt
1 C. Bran Buds
1 C. chocolate chips

Preheat oven to 375°. Cream shortening and sugar. Stir in eggs and vanilla. Sift dry ingredients and add to creamed mixture. Stir in Bran Buds and chips. Drop by teaspoon on greased cookie sheet. Bake for 12 minutes.

PEANUT CHOCOLATE CHIP COOKIES

¼ C. butter or oleo
¼ C. shortening
2 T. peanut butter
½ C. white sugar
½ C. brown sugar
1 egg

1 tsp. vanilla
1⅓ C. flour
½ tsp. baking soda
½ tsp. salt
1 C. salted Spanish peanuts
1-6 oz. pkg. chocolate chips

Preheat oven to 350°. Use electric mixer. Cream shortening, sugars and peanut butter well. Add egg and vanilla. Next, add sifted dry ingredients. Stir well. Then add peanuts and chips. Mix and drop on greased cookie sheet. Bake 8 to 10 minutes. Very good for freezer.

CHOCOLATE NUT REVELS

1 C. butter or margarine
⅔ C. sugar
¼ tsp. salt
1 tsp. vanilla

1 C. chocolate chips
1 C. chopped pecans
2 C. flour

Preheat oven to 350°. Melt chocolate chips over hot water. Add nuts and cool. Thoroughly cream first 4 ingredients. Gradually blend flour into creamed mixture. Add chocolate and nuts. Stir with a fork just enough to revel. Drop by teaspoon onto ungreased cookie sheet. Flatten to ¼" with a glass dipped in sugar. Bake 10 to 12 minutes. Yield: 5 dozen.

GOLD RUSH COOKIES

1 can Eagle Brand milk
1½-6 oz. pkg. chocolate
  chips
2 T. butter

1 C. sifted flour
1 tsp. vanilla
1 C. chopped nuts

Melt butter and chocolate in double boiler. Add milk. Then stir in flour, vanilla and nuts. Mix well and chill. Drop by spoon on well greased cookie sheet. Bake for 15 minutes. These will not seem done. Frost with your favorite chocolate frosting. These are almost like candy. Yield: 3 dozen.

CAKE MIX PRONTO COOKIES

1 pkg. 2 layer size yellow
cake mix (pudding type)
¼ C. butter or margarine,
softened
¼ C. strong brewed coffee,
cooled

1 egg
1-6 oz. pkg. semi-sweet
chocolate pieces
½ C. walnuts

In mixer bowl, combine cake mix, butter, coffee and eggs. Beat until smooth; stir in chocolate pieces and nuts. Drop from well-rounded teaspoons onto greased cookie sheet. Bake at 375° for 12 minutes. Let stand a few minutes before removing. Makes 4½ to 5 dozen.

CHOCOLATE MARSHMALLOW COOKIES

1 C. sugar
½ C. shortening
1 egg
1 tsp. vanilla
¼ C. milk

1¾ C. flour
½ tsp. salt
½ tsp. soda
½ C. cocoa
18 marshmallows, cut in half

Preheat oven to 350°. Blend well sugar, shortening, egg and vanilla. Stir in dry ingredients alternately with milk. Drop by teaspoonfuls on greased cookie sheet. Bake for 8 minutes. Remove from oven and press ½ marshmallow, cut side down, on each cookie. Bake 2 minutes more. Cool and frost with chocolate powdered sugar frosting.

MOCHA COOKIE CRISPS

½ C. honey or corn syrup
1½ tsp. instant coffee
  powder
1-3 oz. pkg. German sweet
  chocolate or 4-1 oz. sqs.
  semi-sweet chocolate

⅓ C. butter or margarine
1 C. quick oatmeal
⅔ C. coconut
½ C. packed brown sugar
¼ C. flour

Preheat oven to 300°. Bring combined honey or coffee to boil in 2-quart saucepan. Add chocolate and butter. Stir over low heat until chocolate melts and mixture is smooth. Remove and add remaining ingredients. Drop by level teaspoonfuls onto greased cookie sheet about 3" apart. Bake for 10 to 12 minutes. Cool 2 minutes on cookie sheet before removing. Yield: 3½ dozen.

ONE BOWL CHOCOLATE COOKIES

2 sqs. chocolate
½ C. butter (1 stick)
1 C. sugar
1 egg, unbeaten
½ C. milk

1½ C. sifted flour
2 tsp. baking powder
¼ tsp. salt
1 tsp. vanilla

Preheat oven to 350°. Melt chocolate in mixing bowl. Add butter and sugar. Cream mixture. Add egg, milk, then flour, baking powder and salt. Then add vanilla. Drop with teaspoon on cookie sheet. Bake for 10 minutes. Frost with powdered sugar butter frosting and add half a walnut. Yield: 3 dozen.

CHOCOLATE NUT WAFERS

1 C. soft shortening	2 sqs. chocolate
1 C. sugar	¾ C. flour
1 egg	½ tsp. salt
1 tsp. vanilla	¾ C. nuts, chopped fine

Preheat oven to 325°. Cream the shortening and sugar. Add the egg, vanilla and melted chocolate. Mix well. Add sifted dry ingredients and finely chopped nuts. Drop by teaspoons 2" apart on a greased cookie sheet. Use a glass with a slightly dampened cloth over bottom to press the dough into flat rounds. Bake for 10 to 12 minutes. Yield: 5 dozen.

TURTLE COOKIES

½ C. oleo
2 sqs. chocolate **or**
  4 T. cocoa
2 eggs

¾ C. sugar
1 C. flour
1 tsp. vanilla
½ tsp. salt

Melt the oleo and chocolate. Stir in egg, sugar, flour, vanilla and salt. Drop by ½ teaspoon onto hot waffle iron, baking several at a time. Will bake in 25 to 30 seconds. Frost when cool.

DATE NUT MACAROONS

2 egg whites
1 C. powdered sugar

1 C. chopped dates
1 C. chopped nuts

Preheat oven to 325°. Beat egg whites until stiff and dry. Add ingredients in order given. Drop by teaspoon on buttered cookie sheet. Bake for 12 to 15 minutes.

STUFFED DATE DROPS

1 lb. dates
70 to 80 walnuts or pecans
¼ C. shortening
¾ C. brown sugar
1 egg

1¼ C. sifted flour
½ tsp. baking powder
½ tsp. soda
¼ tsp. salt
½ C. cultured sour cream

Preheat oven to 375°. Stuff each date with a nut half, set aside. Cream the shortening and gradually add brown sugar. Add the egg and mix well. Combine flour, baking powder, soda and salt. Add dry mixture to the shortening, sugar and egg mixture alternately with sour cream. Stir in dates. Drop on a greased cookie sheet (one date per cookie). Bake 8 to 10 minutes. Cool and top with frosting made by slightly browning ½ cup butter, 3 cups powdered sugar, ¾ teaspoon vanilla. Slowly add enough water until icing is of thin consistency. Yield: 6 dozen.

SOFT SOUR CREAM DATE-NUT COOKIES

2 C. brown sugar, packed
1 C. butter
2 eggs
1 C. sour cream
1 tsp. vanilla
1 tsp. baking soda

½ tsp. salt
1 tsp. cloves
½ tsp. cinnamon
3 C. flour
1½ C. dates, chopped
1 C. nuts, chopped

Preheat oven to 350°. Cream butter and sugar together. Add unbeaten eggs. Mix well. Add sour cream and vanilla. Mix and sift all the dry ingredients together. Add them to the butter mixture. Then add the nuts and dates. Drop by teaspoonfuls on greased cookie sheet. Bake for 12 to 15 minutes. Yield: 5 dozen.

COCONUT DATE BALLS

2 C. nuts	1 C. coconut
1 C. pitted dates	2 eggs, slightly beaten
1 C. brown sugar	1½ C. coconut (topping)

Preheat oven to 350°. Grind nuts and dates. Add brown sugar, coconut and eggs. Mix well. Drop by teaspoons into the 1½ cups coconut. Shape into balls. Bake for 15 minutes.

DIABETIC RAISIN COOKIES

2 eggs, beaten
1½ tsp. Sucaryl
1½ tsp. baking powder
⅓ C. raisins

¼ C. flour
½ C. nuts
1½ C. bread crumbs
 (soybean bread is used)

Combine eggs and Sucaryl and add other ingredients in order given. Bake for 8 to 10 minutes.

GROUND RAISIN COOKIES

1 C. oleo	2½ C. flour
1 lb. brown sugar	1 tsp. soda
3 eggs	2½ C. quick oatmeal
2 tsp. vanilla	2 C. ground raisins
1 tsp. salt	1 C. chopped nuts

Preheat oven to 350°. Cream oleo and sugar. Add eggs and vanilla. Mix well and add sifted dry ingredients. Stir in oatmeal, ground raisins and nuts. Drop by teaspoonfuls on greased cookie sheet. Bake for 12 to 15 minutes.

SOFT RAISIN DROP COOKIES

Cook 1 cup raisins in ¾ cup water until raisins are tender. Add 1 teaspoon soda and cool. Cream well 1 cup shortening and 1½ cups sugar. Add 2 eggs and beat well. Add 3 cups flour and 1 teaspoon baking powder. Thoroughly mix. Add raisins and mix. Drop on cookie sheet and bake. ½ cup nuts may be added if desired. Bake for 10 to 12 minutes. Yield: 4 dozen.

PRIDE OF IOWA COOKIES

1 C. brown sugar
1 C. white sugar
1 C. shortening
2 eggs
2 C. flour
½ tsp. salt

1 tsp soda.
1 tsp. baking powder
1 tsp. vanilla
1 C. coconut
3 C. quick oatmeal
½ C. chopped nuts

Preheat oven to 375°. Blend sugars and shortening. Add beaten eggs. Sift dry ingredients together and add to first mixture. Stir in vanilla, coconut, oats and nuts. Mix well and drop by teaspoonful onto greased cookie sheet. Flatten with bottom of glass dipped in sugar. Bake for 8 minutes.

COCONUT OATMEAL COOKIES

1 C. brown sugar
1 C. white sugar
1 C. shortening
2 eggs
½ tsp. salt
2 C. flour

1 tsp. soda
1 tsp. baking powder
1 tsp. vanilla
3 C. quick cooking oats
1 C. coconut
½ C. chopped nuts

Preheat oven to 375°. Cream sugars and shortening. Add eggs, then the rest of the ingredients. Drop by teaspoonfuls on greased cookie sheet and flatten with a glass or fork. Bake for 10 or 12 minutes. Yield: 5 dozen.

BANANA OATMEAL COOKIES

1½ C. flour
½ tsp. soda
1 tsp. salt
¼ tsp. nutmeg
¾ tsp. cinnamon
1¾ C. quick oatmeal

¾ C. shortening
1 C. brown sugar
1 egg, well beaten
1 C. ripe bananas, mashed
½ C. chopped nuts
1 tsp. vanilla

Preheat oven to 350°. Cream sugar and shortening. Add egg and vanilla and mix. Add dry ingredients, sifted together, and banana. Add oatmeal and nuts. Drop by spoon on greased baking sheet. Bake for 10 to 12 minutes.

OATMEAL MACAROONS

1 C. white sugar
1 C. brown sugar
1 C. Crisco
2 eggs
1 tsp. vanilla
2 C. flour

1 tsp. soda
1 tsp. salt
1 tsp. baking powder
1½ C. rice cereal
1 C. oatmeal (quick)
½ C. nuts

Preheat oven to 350°. Cream shortening, sugars, eggs and vanilla. Sift dry ingredients and mix well. Add cereal, oatmeal and nuts. Drop on greased cookie sheet and press down. Bake 8 to 10 minutes.

OATMEAL CHEWS

2 C. white sugar
1 C. Crisco
2 eggs
2½ C. flour
½ tsp. salt

1 tsp. soda
2 C. raisins, ground
2 C. quick oatmeal
1 tsp. vanilla

Preheat oven to 375°. Cream shortening and sugar. Stir in eggs and vanilla; beat well. Sift dry ingredients and stir in. Mix well. Add ground raisins and oatmeal. Bake for 10 to 12 minutes.

BUTTERSCOTCH OATMEAL COOKIES

1 C. shortening
¾ C. brown sugar
¾ C. white sugar
2 eggs
1 T. hot water
1 tsp. vanilla

1½ C. flour
1 tsp. soda
2 C. quick oatmeal
1-6 oz. pkg. butterscotch
 chips
½ C. chopped nuts

Preheat oven to 375°. Cream shortening and sugars. Add eggs and beat well. Then add hot water and vanilla. Add flour mixed with soda. Next, add oatmeal, nuts and chips. Drop by teaspoons on greased cookie sheet. Bake for 10 to 12 minutes.

OATMEAL APRICOT COOKIES

¾ C. shortening
1 C. sugar
1 egg
1 C. cooked, mashed
 apricots
1¾ C. oats
1½ C. flour

1¼ tsp. soda
½ tsp. salt
¼ tsp. nutmeg
¾ tsp. cinnamon
½ C. chopped nuts

Preheat oven to 375°. Cream shortening and sugar. Add egg and beat well. Stir in apricots. Add dry ingredients and nuts. Mix well. Drop on greased cookie sheet. Bake for 10 minutes. (If canned apricots are used, drain and add ¼ cup more flour.)

COCONUT OATMEAL COOKIES

2 C. quick cooking oatmeal	3 T. milk
⅔ C. flaked coconut	1½ tsp. vanilla
1 C. butter or margarine	1½ C. flour
1 C. sugar	½ tsp. soda
2 eggs	½ tsp. salt

Preheat oven to 400°. In oven, toast oats and coconut until golden brown. Cream butter and sugar. Add eggs, milk and vanilla, beating well. Sift together dry ingredients. Add to creamed mixture, blending well. Stir in oats and coconut. Drop by teaspoon 2" apart on ungreased cookie sheet. Flatten with a glass dipped in sugar. Sprinkle top with untoasted coconut. Bake 8 to 10 minutes. Yield: 4 dozen.

PEANUT BUTTER CRISSCROSSES

1 C. shortening
1 C. granulated sugar
1 C. brown sugar
2 eggs
1 tsp. vanilla

1 C. peanut butter
3 C. flour
2 tsp. soda
½ tsp. salt

Preheat oven to 350°. Cream shortening, sugars, eggs and vanilla. Stir in peanut butter. Sift dry ingredients. Stir into creamed mixture. Drop by rounded teaspoon onto ungreased cookie sheet. Press with fork (dipped in sugar) to make crisscross. Bake for 10 minutes. Yield: 5 dozen.

SALTED PEANUT COOKIES

2 C. flour
1 C. brown sugar
1 C. white sugar
2 eggs, beaten
1 tsp. baking powder
1 scant tsp. baking soda

1 C. salted Spanish
 peanuts, chopped
1 tsp. vanilla
1 C. shortening
1 C. crushed cornflakes
1 C. oatmeal

Preheat oven to 375°. Cream shortening and sugars. Add vanilla and eggs. Cream well. Add cornflakes, oatmeal and sifted dry ingredients. Add nuts. Drop cookies the size of a walnut on greased cookie sheet. Press down with fork. Bake for 14 minutes.

PECAN DAINTIES

1 egg white   1½ C. pecan halves
1 C. light brown sugar

Preheat oven to 250°. Beat egg whites until stiff. Add sugar gradually, beating constantly. Fold in nuts. Drop on greased cookie sheet. Bake for 30 minutes. Yield: 3 to 4 dozen.

SORGHUM DROP COOKIES

1 C. sugar
⅔ C. oleo
1 egg
¼ C. sorghum
2 C. flour

½ tsp. salt
1 tsp. soda
1 tsp. cinnamon
½ tsp. cloves
½ tsp. ginger

Preheat oven to 350°. Cream oleo and sugar. Add egg and sorghum. Mix well. Add dry ingredients and stir well. Drop by teaspoonfuls on greased cookie sheet and press down with fork dipped in sugar. Bake 10 to 12 minutes.

MAPLE NUT DROPS

3 C. and 2 T. sifted flour
1 tsp. baking powder
1 tsp. baking soda
1 tsp. salt
1 C. butter

3 eggs
1 C. maple flavored syrup
¼ tsp. maple flavoring
1 C. cut-up dates
1 C. chopped nuts

Sift all dry ingredients together. Set aside. Cream butter and eggs, maple syrup and flavoring. Blend in dry ingredients. Add ¼ cup boiling water. Mix well. Stir in dates and nuts. Chill at least 1 hour. Drop on greased cookie sheet. Bake for 13 to 16 minutes. Cool and frost with Maple Icing.

MAPLE ICING:
¼ C. butter
2 T. cream
1 tsp. vanilla

1 T. maple flavored syrup
2 C. sifted powdered sugar

Melt butter. Add cream, vanilla and syrup. Blend in powdered sugar. Beat until smooth.

SPICED YUM YUM COOKIES

½ C. shortening
1 C. brown sugar
1 egg
1 C. sour milk
1 C. cut raisins
½ C. chopped nuts
2 C. flour

1 tsp. soda
1 tsp. cinnamon
½ tsp. nutmeg
½ tsp. cloves
1 tsp. lemon flavoring
1 tsp. vanilla

Preheat oven to 325°. Combine shortening, sugar and egg. Mix well. Add the sour milk. Sift the flour, soda and spices. Add the fruit, nuts and flavorings. Bake for 10 to 12 minutes.

50

PERSIMMON COOKIES

¾ C. shortening or oleo
1 C. sugar
1 egg
1 C. seeded persimmons
¼ tsp. soda
2 C. flour

2 tsp. baking powder
¼ tsp. salt
1 T. vanilla
¾ C. nuts
¾ C. coconut

Preheat oven to 375°. Cream sugar and shortening until light and fluffy. Add egg and beat well. Stir soda into persimmons and add to creamed mixture. Add sifted flour, baking powder and salt. Add vanilla, nuts and coconut. Drop on greased cookie sheet. Bake for 12 to 15 minutes. These cookies are good to freeze. Yield: 10 dozen.

PINEAPPLE COOKIES

1 C. brown sugar	4 C. sifted flour
1 C. white sugar	1 tsp. soda
1 C. shortening	1 tsp. vanilla
2 eggs	1 tall (#1) can crushed
1 C. chopped nuts	pineapple, reserve juice

Preheat oven to 350°. Cream sugars and shortening; add eggs, dry ingredients, nuts and vanilla. Fold in crushed pineapple. Drop by teaspoonfuls on greased cookie sheet. Bake for 10 to 12 minutes. Frost while hot with mixture of pineapple juice and powdered sugar. Yield: 5 dozen.

ORANGE COOKIES

Scant ¾ C. shortening
1½ C. brown sugar
2 eggs
1 tsp. vanilla
1½ tsp. grated orange rind

½ C. sour milk
½ tsp. soda
3 C. flour, sifted
1½ tsp. baking powder
¾ C. nutmeats

Preheat oven to 350°. Cream shortening and sugar. Add beaten eggs, vanilla and grated rind. Sift together the dry ingredients and add with the sour milk. Mix well and add chopped nuts. Drop by teaspoons on a greased cookie sheet. Bake for 12 to 15 minutes. While still very hot, spread with the following mixture: 1 cup granulated sugar, ⅓ cup orange juice and 1½ teaspoons grated orange rind. Yield: 5 dozen.

CARROT COOKIES

1 C. shortening (½ butter)
¾ C. sugar
1 egg
1 C. cooked, mashed carrots

1 tsp. vanilla
2 C. sifted flour
1 tsp. baking powder
½ tsp. salt

Cream shortening, sugar, egg, carrots and vanilla. Add flour, baking powder and salt. Drop by teaspoon on greased cookie sheet. Frost while hot. Yield: 4 dozen.

FROSTING: Combine 3 tablespoons orange juice, 1 teaspoon grated orange rind and 2 cups sifted powdered sugar.

PUMPKIN COOKIES

1 C. brown sugar,
  packed firm
1 C. pumpkin
½ C. oil
1 tsp. vanilla
2 C. flour

1 tsp. baking powder
½ tsp. salt
½ tsp. cinnamon
½ tsp. nutmeg
¼ tsp. ginger
1 C. raisins

Preheat oven to 350°. Mix sugar, pumpkin, oil and vanilla. Add sifted dry ingredients and raisins. Drop by teaspoons on well-greased baking sheet. Bake for 15 minutes.

PUMPKIN NUT COOKIES

¼ C. shortening
½ C. sugar
1 egg, beaten
½ C. canned pumpkin
1 C. sifted flour
½ tsp. salt

1 ¼ tsp. cinnamon
¼ tsp. nutmeg
⅛ tsp. ginger
½ C. raisins
½ C. nuts, chopped
Baking powder

Preheat oven to 350°. Cream shortening. Add sugar gradually. Cream until light and fluffy. Add egg and pumpkin. Mix well. Sift flour, baking powder, salt and spices together. Stir in dry ingredients. Mix until blended. Add raisins and nuts. Drop on a greased cookie sheet. Bake about 15 minutes. Yield: 2 dozen.

RICE KRISPIES COOKIES

1 C. shortening	½ tsp. cream of tartar
1 C. sugar	½ tsp. vanilla
1 egg	2 C. flour
½ tsp. soda	2 C. Rice Krispies

Preheat oven to 350°. Combine ingredients in order given. Drop on cookie sheet from a teaspoon. Bake until lightly browned, 10 to 12 minutes. Yield: 4 dozen.

MINCEMEAT DROP COOKIES

¾ C. shortening
1½ C. sugar
3 eggs
1-9 oz. pkg. mincemeat
¼ C. milk

3 C. sifted flour
1 tsp. soda
¾ tsp. salt
1 C. chopped walnuts

Preheat oven to 350°. Cream shortening and sugar; add eggs, one at a time, beating well after each. Finely crumble mincemeat; add to creamed mixture along with milk; stir well. Sift together dry ingredients and stir in. Add nuts. Drop by teaspoons onto greased cookie sheet. Bake about 15 minutes. Yield: 5 dozen.

RANGER COOKIES

½ C. shortening
½ C. white sugar
½ C. brown sugar
1 egg
½ tsp. vanilla
1 C. flour

¼ tsp. baking powder
½ tsp. soda
¼ tsp. salt
1 C. oatmeal
1 C. Wheaties
½ C. coconut

Preheat oven to 375°. Cream shortening and sugars. Add egg and vanilla. Mix dry ingredients together and blend. Add oatmeal, Wheaties and coconut. Mix well and drop on greased cookie sheet. Bake for 15 minutes.

POTATO CHIP COOKIES

1 C. shortening
1 C. brown sugar
1 C. white sugar
2 beaten eggs
1 tsp. vanilla

2 C. flour
1 tsp. soda
2 C. crushed potato chips
1-6 oz. pkg. butterscotch
 chips

Preheat oven to 375°. Cream shortening and sugars. Add eggs and vanilla. Stir in dry ingredients and crushed potato chips. Add butterscotch chips. Drop on greased cookie sheet. Bake for 10 minutes.

60

CRACKER JACK COOKIES

1 C. shortening
1 C. brown sugar
1 C. white sugar
2 eggs
1 tsp. vanilla
1 tsp. baking soda

1 tsp. baking powder
1½ C. flour
1 tsp. salt
2 C. Rice Krispies
2 C. oatmeal
1 C. Spanish peanuts

Preheat oven to 350°. Cream shortening and sugars. Add eggs, vanilla and half the dry ingredients. Add the rest with oatmeal, Rice Krispies and peanuts. Drop by teaspoons on greased cookie sheet. Bake 10 to 12 minutes.

NATURAL CRUNCH COOKIES

1 C. butter
2 C. brown sugar
2 eggs
4½ oz. jar applesauce and
  apricots (baby food) or ½
  C. chopped apples
¼ C. buttermilk
2 tsp. vanilla

4 C. granola, with raisins
  and dates
2 C. flour
1 C. whole-wheat flour
1 tsp. soda
½ tsp. salt
1½ tsp. baking powder
1 tsp. cinnamon

Preheat oven to 350°. Beat butter, eggs and sugar. Blend in baby food, buttermilk and vanilla. Add mixed dry ingredients. Stir well. Stir in granola. Drop on greased cookie sheet. Bake 10 to 12 minutes. Let cool on cookie sheet one minute before removing. Yield: 6 dozen.

MONSTER COOKIES

12 eggs
2 lbs. brown sugar
4 C. sugar
1 T. vanilla
1 T. Karo dark syrup
8 tsp. soda

1 lb. butter
3 lbs. peanut butter
18 C. oatmeal
1 lb. chocolate chips
1 lb. M & M's

Preheat oven to 350°. Cream butters and sugars. Add remainder of ingredients. Drop and flatten on cookie sheet. Bake 10 to 12 minutes.

SHAPED COOKIES

● ●

ALMOND CRESCENTS

1 C. butter
⅓ C. sugar
1⅔ C. flour

⅔ C. ground almonds
¼ tsp. salt
Almond flavoring

Preheat oven to 325°. Cream butter and sugar. Add flour, salt and flavoring. Mix well. Add nuts and blend. Roll in long pencil-like rolls. Form into crescents. Bake for 15 minutes. While warm, dip in powdered sugar.

PECAN PUFFS

½ C. butter
2 T. sugar
1 tsp. vanilla

1 C. pecans, chopped fine
1 C. flour

Preheat oven to 300°. Cream butter and sugar. Add vanilla, pecans and flour. Make the size of walnuts and place on greased cookie sheet. Bake for 15 minutes. Roll in powdered sugar when taken from oven. Cool. Roll again in powdered sugar.

PECAN CRESCENTS

1 C. butter
¾ C. powdered sugar
2 tsp. vanilla
1 tsp. water

2¼ C. flour
1 C. pecans, ground
Powdered sugar

Preheat oven to 325°. Work together first 4 ingredients. Then add mixture of flour and pecans. Shape in crescents and bake until very light, 15 minutes. Roll in powdered sugar.

APPLE CHEESE CRESCENTS

¾ C. butter or margarine
1 C. sugar
½ tsp. vanilla
3 C. flour

½ tsp. salt
1 tsp. cinnamon
½ Cheddar cheese
⅓ C. applesauce

Preheat oven to 350°. Cream butter until light and fluffy. Gradually beat in ½ cup sugar until well blended. Blend in grated cheese, applesauce and vanilla alternately with flour, beating well. On wax paper, combine remaining ½ cup sugar and cinnamon. With hands, shape dough by rounded teaspoonfuls into balls; roll in sugar and cinnamon. Mold crescent shapes. Bake for 12 to 15 minutes. Cool 5 minutes before removing from cookie sheet. Yield: 4 dozen.

COUNTESS COOKIES

1 C. Crisco
¼ C. butter
¾ C. brown sugar
1 beaten egg

2 tsp. vanilla
1½ C. flour
1¼ tsp. baking powder
¾ tsp. salt

Preheat oven to 350°. Cream Crisco, butter and sugar. Add egg and vanilla. Mix well. Mix in dry ingredients. Moisten hands and shape dough into small balls. Roll in quick oatmeal, making as much as possible stick to cookie. Place on greased cookie sheet. Cut maraschino cherries into quarters, then press crosswise, one piece to each cookie. Bake for 12 minutes.

GINGERSNAPS

¾ C. shortening
1 C. brown sugar
¼ C. molasses
1 egg
2¼ C. sifted flour

2 tsp. soda
½ tsp. salt
1 tsp. ginger
1 tsp. cinnamon
½ tsp. cloves

Preheat oven to 375°. Cream together first 4 ingredients until fluffy. Sift together dry ingredients. Stir into molasses mixture. Form in small balls. Roll in sugar. Place 2" apart on greased cookie sheet. Bake about 10 minutes. Cool slightly before removing from pan. Yield: 5 dozen.

●●●●●●●●●●●●●●●●●●●●●●●●●●●●●●●●●

CARDAMON COOKIES

1 C. sugar
1 C. butter
2 C. flour

1 tsp. baking powder
⅔ tsp. cardamon

Preheat oven to 375°. Cream sugar and butter. Add flour, baking powder and cardamon. Mix well. Roll in balls the size of a marble and bake on lightly greased cookie sheet. Watch closely. They burn quickly. Bake for 10 to 12 minutes.

GERMAN SUGAR COOKIES

½ C. oleo
½ C. Crisco
1¼ C. sugar
3 egg yolks
1 tsp. vanilla

½ tsp. lemon extract
2½ to 2¾ C. flour
1 tsp. soda
1 tsp. cream of tartar
1 tsp. salt

Preheat oven to 375°. Cream together shortening and sugar. Add egg yolks, vanilla and lemon. Add sifted dry ingredients. Roll in balls, dip top in sugar and bake until brown.

HERITAGE COOKIES

1 C. soft oleo
1 C. sugar
1 tsp. vanilla
1 C. flour

2 C. quick oatmeal
½t sp. soda
¼ tsp. salt

Preheat oven to 350°. Mix together thoroughly oleo, sugar and vanilla. Sift together and stir in flour, soda and salt. Stir in oatmeal. Shape into balls and press down with glass dipped in sugar. Bake for 8 to 10 minutes.

CHERRY WINKS

¾ C. shortening
1 C. sugar
2 eggs
½ tsp. salt
1 tsp. vanilla
2 T. milk

2¼ C. sifted flour
1 tsp. baking powder
½ tsp. soda
1 C. chopped pecans
1 C. dates, cut fine
⅓ C. maraschino cherries

Preheat oven to 375°. Combine shortening and sugar. Cream well. Add salt, vanilla, milk and eggs. Add sifted dry ingredients and mix well. Fold in fruit and nuts. Roll in balls using 1 tablespoon for each cookie. Bake for 10 to 12 minutes.

SNICKERDOODLES

1 C. soft shortening
1½ C. sugar
2 eggs
2¾ C. flour

2 tsp. cream of tartar
½ tsp. salt
1 tsp. soda

Mix shortening, sugar and eggs together. Sift together remaining ingredients. Blend the 2 mixtures. Chill dough. Roll into balls the size of a walnut. Then roll in mixture of 2 tablespoons sugar, 2 teaspoons cinnamon. Place 2" apart on ungreased cookie sheet. Bake for 8 to 10 minutes. These cookies will puff up at first, then flatten with crinkled top. Yield: 5 dozen.

SNOWBALLS

¾ C. butter
1 tsp. vanilla
1 T. water
⅛ tsp. salt

⅓ C. sugar
1½ C. flour
1-6 oz. pkg. chocolate chips
1 C. chopped nuts

Preheat oven to 300°. Cream butter, vanilla, water, salt and sugar. Add flour into creamed mixture. Add chips and nuts. Form in 1" balls. Place on ungreased cookie sheet. Bake for 20 minutes. Roll in sugar while warm.

CANDY STAR COOKIES

1¾ C. flour	½ C. sugar
1 tsp. soda	½ C. brown sugar
½ tsp. salt	1 egg
½ C. butter	1 tsp. vanilla
⅓ C. peanut butter	1 pkg. chocolate stars

Preheat oven to 375°. Cream butter, peanut butter and sugars. Add egg and dry ingredients and mix well. Shape dough into balls, then roll in sugar. Bake 8 minutes. Remove and place a candy star on top of cookie and press. Put back in oven for 1 minute. Yield: 3 dozen.

PEPPERMINT CHOCOLATE BALLS

½ C. shortening
¼ C. crushed peppermint
 candy stick
1 egg

1 pkg. devil's food cake mix
Powdered sugar
Finely chopped walnuts

Preheat oven to 350°. Mix shortening and egg until well blended and add candy. Add cake mix and work with fingers. Form into balls, about 1½". Bake for about 10 minutes and remove from cookie sheet immediately. Sprinkle with powdered sugar and nuts, if desired. Yield: 3 dozen.

CHOCOLATE MELTAWAYS

2 C. cake flour
⅛ tsp. salt
¾ C. butter
1 C. sugar
½ tsp. vanilla

1 egg
2 T. milk
2 sqs. unsweetened
  chocolate (2 oz.)
⅓ C. finely chopped walnuts
5 tsp. sweet cocoa beverage
  mix

Cream butter, sugar and vanilla. Beat egg until thick. Beat into creamed mixture. Add chocolate melted in milk. Gradually add flour and salt mixed together. Turn out on wax paper. Shape into rectangle with a spatula. Cover and freeze firm. Cut into 4 portions. Remove one portion at a time. Shape into 18 balls. Roll in nuts mixed with cocoa mix. Place on ungreased cookie sheet. Bake at 375° for 10 minutes. Yield: 6 dozen.

NUTMEG COOKIES

1 C. oleo
2 tsp. vanilla
3 tsp. rum flavoring
¾ C. sugar
1 egg
3 C. flour
2 tsp. nutmeg
¼ tsp. salt

FROSTING:
⅓ C. oleo
1 tsp. vanilla
2 tsp. rum flavoring
2 C. sifted powdered sugar
1 T. cream

Preheat oven to 350°. Cream oleo, vanilla, flavoring and sugar. Add eggs. Beat well. Sift and add flour, nutmeg and salt. On sugared board, shape dough into roll ½" in diameter. Cut into 3" lengths. Place on ungreased cookie sheet. Bake for 15 minutes. Cool. Frost with frosting. Sprinkle with nutmeg after you frost.

80

HONEY SUNDIES

1 C. shortening
2 C. flour
¼ C. honey

½ tsp. vanilla or almond
 extract
½ tsp. salt
2 C. pecans, chopped

**Preheat oven to 300°. Cream shortening. Add honey and extract. Mix well.
Add sifted dry ingredients. Blend in nuts. Roll in small balls. Bake for 30
minutes. Roll in powdered sugar while still hot and again when cooled.
Yield: 30 cookies.**

DELICIOUS OATMEAL COOKIES

1 C. butter
1½ C. sugar
1 C. cottage cheese
2 eggs
1 tsp. baking powder
½ tsp. soda
1 tsp. vanilla

¼ tsp. salt
2 tsp. cinnamon
2 C. quick oatmeal
1 C. raisins
½ C. nuts
2 C. flour

Preheat oven to 375°. Cream butter and sugar. Add cottage cheese and eggs. Mix well. Stir in dry ingredients. Add oatmeal, raisins, vanilla and nuts. Stir until well blended. Roll dough into balls. Dip in sugar. Bake for 10 to 15 minutes.

DATE COOKIES

1 C. sugar
1 C. shortening
2 eggs, beaten
2 T. milk
2 C. flour
½ tsp. soda

1 tsp. baking powder
¼ tsp. salt
1 tsp. vanilla
1 C. chopped dates
1 C. chopped nuts
Crushed cornflakes

Preheat oven to 350°. Cream shortening and sugar until fluffy. Add beaten eggs and vanilla. Mix well. Add flour, soda, baking powder and salt alternately with milk. Add dates and nuts. Make into balls and dip into crushed cornflakes. Bake for 15 to 20 minutes.

ORANGE CANDY COOKIES

1½ C. brown sugar
½ C. shortening
2 eggs
2 C. sifted flour
1 tsp. soda
½ tsp. baking powder

½ tsp. salt
1 lb. orange slice candy,
  diced and mixed with
½ C. flour
½ C. flaked coconut
½ C. chopped nuts
½ C. rolled oats

Preheat oven to 325°. Cream sugar and shortening until light and fluffy. Beat in eggs. Sift flour, soda, baking powder and salt and blend into creamed mixture. Fold in candy, coconut, nuts and rolled oats, mixing well. Roll into balls, about 1" in diameter. Place on greased baking sheet and press down with a fork. Bake for 12 minutes or until lightly browned. Yield: 6 dozen.

SANDIES

1 C. butter or margarine
⅓ C. sugar
2 tsp. water

2 tsp. vanilla
2 C. sifted flour
1 C. chopped pecans

Cream butter and sugar. Add water and vanilla. Mix well. Add flour and pecans. Chill 3 or 4 hours. Shape into balls or fingers. Bake on ungreased cookie sheet at 325° about 20 minutes. Cool slightly. Roll in powdered sugar. Yield: 3 dozen.

CEREAL COOKIES

1 C. shortening
1 C. brown sugar
¾ C. white sugar
2 eggs
2 C. oatmeal
2 C. coconut
2 C. Rice Krispies

1 tsp. vanilla
1 tsp. salt
2 C. flour
½ tsp. soda
1 tsp. baking powder
½ C. nuts

Preheat oven to 375°. Cream shortening and sugars. Add beaten eggs. Stir in oatmeal, salt, flour, soda, baking powder and nuts. Fold in coconut, Rice Krispies and vanilla. Form into small balls and press down with glass dipped in sugar. Bake for 12 to 15 minutes.

LOW CHOLESTEROL COOKIES

3¼ C. oatmeal   ¾ C. corn oil margarine
¾ C. sugar   1 tsp. vanilla

Preheat oven to 350°. Mix all ingredients together with hands. Form 1" balls and place on ungreased baking sheet. Flatten with fork dipped in water. Bake for 12 to 15 minutes. Let stand for 1 minute before removing from cookie sheet.

REFRIGERATED COOKIES

ICEBOX COOKIES

1½ C. shortening
  (part butter)
2 C. brown sugar
3 eggs
5 C. flour

1 tsp. cinnamon
1 tsp. soda
¼ tsp. salt
½ C. chopped nuts

Cream shortening and sugar together. Add well-beaten eggs. Mix dry ingredients and add gradually to creamed shortening. Add nuts. Roll into 2 rolls. Let stand in refrigerator overnight. Slice thin and bake at 400° for 15 minutes.

ORANGE ICEBOX COOKIES

1 C. brown sugar
1 C. white sugar
1 C. butter or oleo
3 eggs
1 tsp. salt
1 tsp. vanilla

1 tsp. lemon extract
Grated rind of 1 orange
1 C. dates, cut fine
1 C. nutmeats
4 C. flour
2 tsp. soda

Cream together thoroughly butter, sugars, eggs, vanilla, lemon flavoring and orange rind. Sift together dry ingredients and add to first mixture. Stir in dates and nuts. Shape into roll and refrigerate overnight. Cut in thin slices and bake 375° 12 to 15 minutes.

SUGAR COOKIES
(CUT OUT COOKIES)

2 C. sifted flour
½ tsp. baking powder
½ tsp. soda
½ tsp. salt
⅔ C. butter **or** margarine

1 C. sugar
1 egg, beaten
2 T. milk
½ tsp. vanilla
½ tsp. lemon extract

Sift first 4 ingredients together. Cream butter and sugar. Blend in egg, milk and flavorings. Blend in dry ingredients. Chill in refrigerator 2 hours. Roll ⅛" thick on lightly floured board. Cut into desired shapes with floured cookie cutters. Bake on ungreased cookie sheet at 350° for 10 to 12 minutes. Yield: 5 dozen.

ICE CREAM COOKIES

1 C. sugar
1 C. butter or margarine
2 egg yolks
2 C. flour

2 tsp. vanilla
¼ tsp. salt
Sugar **and** finely chopped
  nutmeats for dipping

Preheat oven to 350°. Cream butter and sugar. Add egg yolks, vanilla, flour and salt. Mix until well blended. Roll in small balls. Dip in sugar and nuts. Place on greased cookie sheet. Press with glass. Bake at 350° about 8 minutes until very delicately browned on edges. Yield: 4 dozen.

APPLESAUCE ICEBOX COOKIES

1½ C. shortening
2 C. sugar
1 beaten egg
4½ to 5 C. flour
¼ tsp. salt
1 tsp. soda

1 tsp. cinnamon
½ tsp. cloves
1 C. unsweetened
    applesauce
1 C. chopped nuts

Cream together shortening and sugar. Add egg. Sift dry ingredients and fold into creamed mixture alternately with applesauce. Add nuts and mix into stiff dough. Form into 2 rolls and wrap in wax paper and stove in refrigerator. Slice thin and bake at 375° for 15 to 20 minutes.

PEPERNUTS

1 C. margarine
1½ C. brown sugar
1 egg yolk
6 T. cream

1 tsp. cinnamon
¼ tsp. ginger
⅛ tsp. cloves
3 C. flour

Cream margarine and sugar. Add yolk and cream. Mix well. Then add dry ingredients. Chill and form into pencil-like rolls. Freeze and slice in ¼" slices. Bake at 350° for 10 minutes.

COFFEE AND SPICE DROPS

1 C. soft shortening
2 C. brown sugar
2 eggs
½ C. cold coffee
3½ C. flour

1 tsp. soda
1 tsp. salt
1 tsp. nutmeg
1 tsp. cinnamon

Preheat oven to 400°. Mix together shortening, sugar and eggs. Stir in coffee. Sift dry ingredients and stir into creamed mixture. Chill at least 1 hour. Drop rounded teaspoonfuls about 2" apart on lightly greased cookie sheet. Bake for 8 to 10 minutes. Yield: 6 dozen.

PECAN ROUNDS

1 C. butter
½ C. sugar
1 tsp. vanilla

⅛ tsp. salt
2 C. flour
1 C. ground pecans

Preheat oven to 350°. Mix butter, sugar and vanilla until creamy. Add flour and salt and mix well. Last, add pecans and mix. Make in rolls and freeze. When needed, slice and bake until set.

SOFT MOLASSES COOKIES

1 C. shortening	2 T. vinegar
1 C. brown sugar	5 C. flour
2 eggs	1 T. ginger
1 C. molasses	1 T. soda

Cream sugar and shortening. Add remaining ingredients. Refrigerate 3 to 4 hours. Roll in balls and place on cookie sheet. Press with sugared glass. Bake at 325° about 10 minutes. Frost with powdered sugar frosting.

MOLASSES CRINKLES

¾ C. soft shortening
1 C. brown or white sugar
1 egg
¼ C. molasses
2¼ C. sifted flour

2 tsp. soda
¼ tsp. salt
½ tsp. cloves
1 tsp. ginger
1 tsp. cinnamon

Mix thoroughly shortening, sugar, egg and molasses. Sift together remaining ingredients and stir in. Chill dough. Will keep for several days. Form into balls size of large walnut. Place about 2" apart. Bake at 375° for 12 minutes. Yield: 4 dozen.

CRISP OATMEAL COOKIES

1 C. shortening	1½ C. flour
1 C. brown sugar	1 tsp. salt
1 C. white sugar	1 tsp. soda
2 eggs, beaten	3 C. quick oatmeal
2 tsp. vanilla	½ C. chopped nuts

Combine shortening and sugars and mix well. Add eggs and vanilla. Combine dry ingredients and add to creamed mixture. Add oatmeal and mix well. Then mix in nuts. Make dough into roll and chill. Cut in slices and bake at 350° for 10 minutes. When cool, frost.

FROSTING: Six tablespoons butter, 1½ cups powdered sugar and 1 teaspoon water. Cook butter until light brown. Remove from stove and add the powdered sugar and water. Beat well.

OATMEAL COOKIES

1 C. brown sugar	1½ C. flour
1 C. white sugar	1 tsp. soda
1 C. Crisco	1 tsp. salt
2 eggs	3 C. oatmeal
1 tsp. vanilla	½ C. pecans

Cream shortening and sugars. Add eggs and vanilla. Mix well. Add dry ingredients and mix thoroughly. Add oatmeal and pecans. Form into rolls. Chill. Slice and bake at 350° for 10 to 12 minutes.

SAND TARTS

½ C. butter
1 C. sugar
2 egg yolks, beaten
1 T. milk
½ tsp. vanilla

1½ C. flour
1 tsp. baking powder
½ tsp. salt
Almonds, egg whites,
   sugar and cinnamon

Cream butter and sugar. Add egg yolks, milk and vanilla. Beat until light. Sift together flour, baking powder and salt. Add to first mixture. Chill several hours. Roll thin and cut with a 3" star cutter. Place on greased cookie sheet and put a split blanched almond on each. Brush with unbeaten egg white, then sprinkle with mixture of 1 tablespoon sugar and ½ teaspoon cinnamon. Bake at 375° for 10 minutes.

BONBONS

1 C. butter
1½ C. confectioners' sugar
1 beaten egg
½ tsp. vanilla

½ tsp. almond extract
2½ C. flour
1 tsp. soda
1 tsp. cream of tartar

Cream butter and sugar. Add egg and extracts, beating well. Add sifted dry ingredients and mix thoroughly. Chill for 1 hour. Form into small balls, place on greased cookie sheet and flatten slightly. Center each with an almond. Bake at 375° for 10 to 12 minutes.

TOLL HOUSE CRUNCH COOKIES

1 C. butter or margarine
¾ C. light brown sugar,
 packed
¾ C. sugar
2 eggs, beaten
2¼ C. sifted flour
1 tsp. salt

1 tsp. baking soda
1 tsp. hot water
1-12 oz. pkg. semi-sweet
 chocolate chips
1 C. chopped nuts
1 tsp. vanilla

Preheat oven to 375°. Cream butter with an electric mixer at medium speed. Gradually beat in sugars, then eggs, beating until very light and fluffy. Sift flour with salt. Dissolve baking soda in hot water. Add flour to butter mixture alternately with soda. Stir in chocolate chips, nuts and vanilla. Refrigerate dough, covered, overnight. Roll a teaspoon of dough to form balls and press flat with fingertips. Bake for 10 to 12 minutes. Yield: 8 dozen.

CHOCOLATE ICEBOX COOKIES

2 C. sifted flour
1¾ tsp. baking powder
½ tsp. salt
½ C. butter or oleo
¾ C. sugar

1 egg
2 sqs. baking chocolate
1 tsp. vanilla
¾ C. chopped nuts

Cream butter and sugar. Add egg and beat well. Blend in chocolate and vanilla. Add flour sifted with baking powder and salt. Add nuts. Roll in 2 rolls 2" in diameter. Chill. Slice and bake at 350°.

CHOCOLATE DROP COOKIES

½ C. shortening
1⅔ C. sugar
2 tsp. vanilla
2 eggs, beaten
2 sqs. chocolate, melted
2 C. flour

2 tsp. baking powder
½ tsp. salt
⅓ C. milk
½ C. chopped nuts
Powdered sugar

Preheat oven to 350°. Cream the shortening and sugar. Add eggs, vanilla, chocolate and remaining ingredients except powdered sugar and mix well. Chill for 3 hours. Form into small balls and roll in powdered sugar. Bake for 10 minutes.

105

WASHBOARDS

1 C. shortening (half butter)
2 C. brown sugar
2 eggs
¼ C. water
1 tsp. vanilla

4 C. sifted flour
1½ tsp. baking powder
½ tsp. soda
¼ tsp. salt
1 C. shredded coconut

Mix together thoroughly shortening, sugar and eggs. Stir in water and vanilla. Sift together and stir in dry ingredients. Mix in coconut. Chill dough 2 hours. Roll into balls the size of a walnut. Place 2" apart on ungreased cookie sheet with fingers, flatten each cookie ball into a 1½x2½" oblong, ¼" thick. Press each cookie lengthwise with fork dipped in sugar. Bake at 400° for 8 to 10 minutes. Yield: 5 dozen.

HOLIDAY FRUIT COOKIES

1 C. soft shortening
2 C. brown sugar
2 eggs
½ C. sour milk or
  buttermilk
3½ C. sifted flour

1 tsp. soda
1 tsp. salt
1½ C. broken pecans
2 C. candied cherries,
  cut in halves
2 C. dates

Preheat oven to 400°. Thoroughly cream shortening, sugar and eggs. Stir in milk. Sift and stir in dry ingredients. Mix into dough: nuts, cherries and dates. Chill 1 hour. Drop small teaspoonfuls on greased cookie sheet. Place a pecan half on each cookie. Bake for 8 to 10 minutes. Yield: 6½ dozen.

CARAMEL COOKIES

4 C. brown sugar
1 C. butter
5 eggs
1 tsp. soda
2 tsp. cream of tartar

1 tsp. vanilla
7 C. flour
1 tsp. salt
2 C. nutmeats

Cream butter and sugar. Beat eggs and add other ingredients, mixing well and adding nutmeats last. Roll into 2 long rolls and let stand overnight. Slice and bake as wanted. Bake at 350° for 10 to 12 minutes. It is necessary to use butter instead of shortening.

BLACK WALNUT DROP COOKIES

½ C. shortening
½ C. oleo
1 C. white sugar
½ C. packed brown sugar
2 eggs
2 tsp. vanilla
½ tsp. maple extract
¼ tsp. black walnut extract
¼ tsp. butter flavoring

3½ C. flour
1 tsp. salt
1 tsp. soda
¼ C. dates, cut up
½ raisins
1 C. coconut
½ C. nuts
6 oz. chocolate chips

Cream shortenings, sugars and eggs. Add flavorings and mix. Add dry ingredients mixed together. Then add dates, raisins, coconut, nuts and chips. Mix one day, refrigerate and bake the next day at 375° for 12 minutes.

BITE-SIZE COOKIES
(LOW-CALORIE)

1 ½ tsp. liquid sweetener
1 ½ tsp. baking powder
2 eggs, beaten
⅓ C. dates

¼ C. flour
½ C. chopped nuts
1 ½ C. bread crumbs

Mix sweetener and baking powder. Add eggs and blend. Add flour, dates, nuts and crumbs. Mix well. Refrigerate ½ hour. Drop on greased cookie sheet and bake at 350° for 10 minutes.

GUMDROP COOKIES

1 C. shortening
2 C. brown sugar
2 eggs
½ C. water

3½ C. flour
1 tsp. soda
1 tsp. salt
3 C. cut-up gumdrops

Cream shortening and sugar. Add eggs, one at a time, beating well. Mix dry ingredients together and mix alternately with water. Last, add gumdrops. Chill 1 hour. Drop on greased cookie sheet. Bake at 400° for 10 minutes.

FILLED COOKIES

FILLED COOKIES

1 C. sugar
1 C. shortening
1 egg
⅛ tsp. salt
3½ C. flour
½ C. sweet milk
1 tsp. vanilla
2 tsp. cream of tartar

1½ tsp. soda
FILLING:
1 C. raisins or dates, cut up
1 T. flour
½ C. sugar
½ C. water
½ nuts

Preheat oven to 375°. Cream shortening and sugar. Add slightly beaten egg and vanilla, mixing well. Add milk. Sift dry ingredients together and add to mixture. Roll out thin and cut in rounds.

FILLING: Mix flour and sugar together. Add raisins or dates and water and boil together. Add nuts, if desired. Cool mixture before filling cookies. Place filling between 2 rounds and seal the cookies together with fork. Bake until very light brown.

113

WHOOPEE PIE

½ C. melted shortening
1 C. sugar
3 sqs. melted chocolate
2 eggs
½ C. milk

2⅓ C. flour
1 tsp. baking powder
1 tsp. soda
¼ tsp. salt

Preheat oven to 350°. Mix sugar and shortening. Add melted chocolate and eggs. Add milk alternately with sifted dry ingredients. Drop on greased cookie sheet. Bake 10 minutes. Cool. Spread filling between two cookies. Yield: 24 cookies.

FILLING:
4 heaping T. flour   *½ C. butter*
1 C. milk   *1 C. vegetable shortening*

Cook flour and milk until thick. Cool. Cream butter and shortening. Add the cooled flour-milk mixture to the creamed butter and sugar. Beat with mixer until very creamy.

JELLY JEWEL COOKIES

½ C. butter
¼ C. brown sugar
1 egg, separated

1 C. flour
½ C. finely chopped pecans
1 small jar currant or
   raspberry jelly

Cream butter and sugar together until fluffy. Add well-beaten egg yolk. Stir in flour. Chill dough. Roll in small balls. Dip in slightly-beaten egg whites, then into finely chopped pecans. Place on cookie sheet. Bake at 360° 5 minutes. Remove, make a depression in center of each ball, and return to oven for 10 minutes. Cool. When cold, drop a small amount of jelly in center of each cookie. Yield: 2 dozen.

RAISIN FILLED COOKIES

2 C. brown sugar
1 C. shortening (Crisco or
  butter)
3 eggs, beaten

1 tsp. soda, dissolved in
  1 T. water)
3½ C. flour or more, to
  make a soft dough

Preheat oven to 375°. Cream sugar and shortening together. Add beaten eggs. Add dissolved soda. Add flour to make a soft dough. Roll out ¼" thick and cut with a cookie cutter. Add 1 teaspoon filling and place another cookie on top. Bake for 20 minutes. Yield: 3½ dozen.

FILLING:
1 C. raisins
1 C. sugar

2 T. cornstarch
1 C. water

Mix all ingredients together and boil until thick.

MELTING MOMENTS

1 C. oleo   2 C. flour
⅓ C. powdered sugar

Preheat oven to 350°. Cream oleo and sugar until fluffy. Blend in flour gradually. Beat at medium speed on electric mixer for 5 minutes until satin smooth. Chill several hours. Roll ½ teaspoons into marble-sized balls. Bake on ungreased cookie sheet at 350° for 12 minutes. Put 2 cookies together with frosting.
FROSTING: Blend 1½ cups powdered sugar, 3 tablespoons oleo, 2 tablespoons cream, ¼ teaspoon almond flavoring. Yield: 6 dozen.

DATE PINWHEELS

2¼ C. dates	½ tsp. salt
1 C. water	2 C. brown sugar
1 C. sugar	1 C. shortening
1 C. chopped nuts	2 eggs, well beaten
4 C. flour	½ tsp. soda

Cook dates, water and sugar until thick. Cream shortening and brown sugar. Add eggs and beat well. Add remaining ingredients and beat thoroughly. Divide mixture in 2 equal parts. Roll out separately into rectangular shape, about ¼" thick. Spread with date filling and roll in 2 rolls (long shape). Chill overnight. Slice with sharp knife ¼" thick. Bake for 10 to 12 minutes. Yield: 5 dozen.

DATED FILLED COOKIES

1 C. brown sugar
1 C. shortening
1 egg
2½ C. oatmeal
2¼ C. flour
½ C. hot water
1 tsp. soda

¼ tsp. salt
1 tsp. vanilla
FILLING:
1 lb. dates
½ C. water
½ C. sugar

Cream shortening and sugar. Add egg and beat well. Add oatmeal, water and vanilla. Add remaining ingredients. Chill dough 1 hour. Roll in balls and press down with sugared glass. Bake 10 to 12 minutes. Cool. Cook filling very slowly until dates are tender and spreading consistency. Cool. Put 2 cookies together with filling. Store in airtight containers.

NO BAKE COOKIES

ALMOND BARK COOKIES

1½ lbs. almond bark
1 C. peanut butter
2 C. miniature marshmallows

2 C. salted peanuts
4 C. Rice Krispies

Melt bark in double boiler. Add peanut butter. Stir well. Take off heat. Pour over marshmallows, peanuts and Rice Krispies (which have been mixed in a large bowl) and stir well. Spread in a jellyroll pan or drop by teaspoons on wax paper.

NO BAKE COOKIES

½ C. cocoa
2 C. sugar
½ C. light cream

1½ C. butter or oleo
2 T. light syrup

Mix above ingredients. Boil about 2 minutes. Add 1 teaspoon vanilla. Remove from heat and add quickly 1 cup coconut and 3 cups quick cooking oatmeal. Drop by teaspoons on waxed paper.

CHOCOLATE OATMEAL CRISPS

½ C. butter or margarine
½ C. milk
2 C. sugar
¼ C. cocoa

¼ C. peanut butter
1 ½ tsp. vanilla
½ tsp. salt
2 C. quick cooking oatmeal

In large saucepan, melt butter. Add milk, sugar and cocoa. Stir over medium heat until sugar is dissolved. Bring to a boil and boil for 3 minutes. Remove from heat and blend in peanut butter, vanilla, salt and oatmeal. Drop the warm mixture by teaspoons on a wax paper. Store in airtight container. Yield: 6 dozen.

NO BAKE DATE COOKIES

1 C. dates, cut in half
1½ T. water
1 egg, beaten

¼ C. sugar
2 C. Rice Krispies
½ C. black walnuts

Cook dates, water, egg and sugar until thick. Then add Rice Krispies and black walnuts. Butter hands and roll dough into balls and then roll balls in angel coconut.

124

HOPSCOTCHERS

1-6 oz. pkg. butterscotch
  chips
½ C. peanut butter

2 C. chow mein noodles
2 C. miniature
  marshmallows

Melt chips over double boiler. Stir in peanut butter. Add noodles and marshmallows. Stir well. Drop on waxed paper and chill until set. Yield: 30 cookies.

PEANUT BUTTER BALLS

1⅓ sticks margarine
1 C. peanut butter
1 lb. powdered sugar

6 oz. chocolate chips
1/5 bar paraffin

Mix margarine, peanut butter and powdered sugar. Form into small balls. Melt chocolate chips and paraffin in top of double boiler. Use 2 forks to dip balls in chocolate. Yield: 4 dozen.

PEANUT BUTTER CUPS

2 C. peanut butter
1 stick margarine
1 lb. box powdered sugar

½ tsp. vanilla
1 large (12 oz.) pkg.
 chocolate chips
Paraffin wax

Make centers by mixing oleo, sugar, peanut butter and vanilla. Roll these in small balls and dip in chocolate mixture. (Melt chocolate chips and wax together.) Cool on wax paper.

CORNFLAKE TIDBITS

2 pkgs. butterscotch chips   6 C. cornflakes
⅓ C. peanut butter

Melt chips and peanut butter together in double boiler over low heat. When completely melted, pour over cornflakes and mix thoroughly. Drop by small teaspoonful onto waxed paper and let stand until cool.

CHERRY NUT BALLS

1 C. soft butter or margarine
1 C. sifted powdered sugar
1 tsp. vanilla
½ C. chopped, candied
  cherries

¾ C. coconut
2 C. quick oatmeal
Chopped nutmeats

Beat butter and sugar until creamy. Add vanilla, cherries and coconut. Mix well. Stir in rolled oats. Refrigerate dough for 3 hours. Shape into balls and roll in chopped nuts. Store in refrigerator. Yield: 3 dozen.

CHOW MEIN COOKIES

2 pkgs. butterscotch chips   1 C. pecans or cashews
1 can chow mein noodles

Melt butterscotch chips. Mix in noodles and nuts. Drop by teaspoon on buttered wax paper. Store in cool place.

SPECIALTY COOKIES

JELLY FILLED SWEDISH COOKIES

¼ C. shortening
¼ C. sugar
1 C. sifted flour
1 egg white, unbeaten

½ tsp. vanilla
¼ C. butter
1 egg yolk, slightly beaten
¾ C. chopped nuts

Preheat oven to 350°. Cream butter and shortening. Add sugar and mix well. Add egg yolk and vanilla and blend. Stir in flour. Form into walnut-sized balls. Dip in egg white and roll in nuts. Bake 5 minutes. Remove and make a hole in top of each cookie with thimble. Return to oven and bake 15 minutes more. Fill hole with jelly.

SWEDISH COOKIES

⅔ C. shortening
⅔ C. butter or oleo, soft
1 C. white sugar
1 C. brown sugar, packed
2 eggs
2 tsp. vanilla

3½ C. flour
1 tsp. soda
1 tsp. salt
1 C. nuts, chopped
1-12 oz. pkg. semi-sweet
  chocolate chips

Preheat oven to 350°. Mix thoroughly shortening, butter, sugars, eggs and vanilla. Blend in remaining ingredients. Drop dough by rounded teaspoonful 2" apart onto ungreased cookie sheet. Bake 12 minutes. Yield: 7 dozen.

132

NORWEGIAN KRINGLE

2 C. sour cream (use thick
cream, which has been
soured, not commercial
sour cream)
1 C. sour milk

2 C. sugar
1 tsp. salt
4 to 5 C. flour
to make a soft dough

Preheat oven to 400°. Mix first 4 ingredients, then add flour, a cup at a time. Take a generous tablespoon in fingers and roll like a rope and shape into figure eights. Bake for 10 minutes. Yield: 5 dozen.

133

JAMAICAN COCONUT COOKIES

¼ C. butter
1 C. sugar
2 cans flaked coconut
2 eggs, beaten
1½ C. flour

½ tsp. salt
3 tsp. baking powder
1 tsp. allspice
½ tsp. ginger

Preheat oven to 400°. Cream butter and sugar. Add coconut and eggs. Mix well. Add flour plus remaining ingredients. Drop by teaspoon onto greased cookie sheet. Bake 8 to 10 minutes. Yield: 5 dozen.

MEXICAN WEDDING CAKE COOKIES

½ C. soft butter
3 T. powdered sugar
1 C. cake flour

¾ C. chopped pecans
1 tsp. vanilla

Preheat oven to 350°. Mix butter and sugar. Add flour and mix well. Add nuts and vanilla. Shape in balls and place on cookie sheet. Bake 12 minutes. Do not overbake. These cookies will not get brown. Roll in powdered sugar while hot.

SPRITZ COOKIES

1 C. butter
1¼ C. light brown sugar
1 egg

1 tsp. vanilla
2½ C. flour
1 tsp. baking powder

Preheat oven to 325°. Cream sugar, butter, egg and vanilla. Mix flour and baking powder together and add to creamed mixture. shape with a cookie press. Place on ungreased cookie sheet and bake at 325° until light brown. Yield: 2 dozen.

BEST SPRITZ COOKIES

1 C. butter
⅔ C. sugar
3 egg yolks

2½ C. flour
¼ tsp. almond extract

Preheat oven to 350°. Cream butter and sugar. Add egg yolks. Mix well. Add flour and extract. Put through spritz cookie machine. Bake about 10 minutes.

HOLIDAY COOKIES

3 C. vanilla wafers
1 can Eagle Brand milk

⅓ C. rum (or artificial
  flavoring)
1 C. chopped nuts

Roll vanilla wafers very fine. Combine crumbs with nuts and milk. Add rum.
Blend well and chill for 1 hour. Dip hands in powdered sugar and roll
cookies into small balls and let ripen a few days. (These keep well.)

LACE COOKIES

2 eggs, separate
2 C. Quaker oats
1 C. sugar
2 tsp. baking powder

½ tsp. salt
1 tsp. vanilla
1 T. butter

Preheat oven to 350°. Beat egg yolks and add oats, sugar, baking powder, salt, vanilla and butter. Mix well. Add beaten whites of eggs last. Put ½ teaspoon far apart on lightly greased cookie sheet. Bake about 8 to 10 minutes.

NOTES • NOTES • NOTES • NOTES • NOTES

UNI-Cookbook Categories

1100	Cookies	3400	Low Cholesterol
1200	Casseroles	3500	Chocoholic
1300	Meat Dishes	3700	Cajun
1400	Microwave	3800	Household Hints
1500	Cooking for "2"	6100	Chinese Recipes
1600	Slow Cooking	6400	German Recipes
1700	Low Calorie	6700	Italian Recipes
1900	Pastries & Pies	6800	Irish Recipes
2000	Charcoal Grilling	7000	Mexican Recipes
2100	Hors D'oeuvres	7100	Norwegian Recipes
2200	Beef	7200	Swedish Recipes
2300	Holiday Collections		
2400	Salads & Dressings		
2500	How to Cook Wild Game		
2600	Soups		
3100	Seafood & Fish		
3200	Poultry		
3300	My Own Recipes		

Available Titles 1/94

Titles change without notice.

G&R
Publishing Co.
507 Industrial Street
Waverly, IA 50677